TIMESCAPE
AND OTHER CARIBBEAN POEMS

BY

LANCE BANNISTER
AND
MARCIA HAROLD HINDS

KINGS-SVG PUBLISHERS

PUBLISHED BY

KINGS-SVG PUBLISHERS
BOX 2713, ST. VINCENT AND THE GRENADINES
AND
BOX 702, MADISON, NJ 07940, USA
kingba@aol.com
www.kingsinn-svg.com

**TIMESCAPE
AND OTHER CARIBBEAN POEMS**

ISBN: 0-9778981-4-8

PUBLICATION DATE: AUGUST 2009

EDITORS: BALDWIN KING AND CHERYL L. A. KING

PRINTED IN THE USA

COVER: "SUNFLOWER TIME" IRON SCULPTURE, BARBADOS.
SCULPTOR: LANCE BANNISTER
PHOTOGRAPHER: JASON CORBIN

ACKNOWLEDGEMENTS

Lance Bannister would like to thank Nailah Imojah for her meticulous yet imaginative proof-reading; Ricardo Brewster for expanding the horizons; .Charlie and Grace Pilgrim for reading and appreciating; Martin Hughes and Sandra Gale of Lashley Enterprises for photocopying; Howard and Jill Griffith for the vision and the dream and Baldwin and Cheryl King for tolerance, forbearance and the will to make it work.

DEDICATION

Lance Bannister:
To my wife Joyce and family who stood with me through thick and thin.

Marcia Harold Hinds:
To my husband Patrick with love

TABLE OF CONTENTS

PART A – TIMESCAPE 7

1. Sculptor Time 9
2. Bus Driver Time 10
3. Refine Time 11
4. Shopkeeper Time 12
5. Bogeyman Time 14
6. Schoolmaster Time 15
7. Old Bridge-Player Time ..16
8. Bird On the Wing Time 19
9. Clocks 20
10. Timescape 22
11. Evening Garden 23

ALL SEEING EYE 26

12. Philosophy 27
13. Kamau 30
14. The Dump 33
15. T.V.Holic 34
16. Identity Crisis 35
17. Perverse Generation 36
18. Equus   37
19. The Tree 39
20. Village 40
21. Banjoman 41
22. Barbados Day 43
23. Baxter Road Awakes 47
24. Baxter Road 48
25. Baxter Road 2 49
26. Baxter's Road A La Carte 50
27. Cries of the Marketplace 51
28. Rufus the Cock 52
29. Circe 54
30. Cole's Cave 55
31. Bush Doctors 56
32. Saturday Night 57
33. Brittons Hill Cave-In 58
34. Moonlight and Morning   59
35. Speightstown 1 60
36. Speightstown 2 61

6 TIMESCAPE AND OTHER CARIBBEAN POEMS

PART B – POETRY AS COMPANY 63

37. Evening Themes 65
38. I Write not Bitter, Biting Ryhme 67
39. Dew at Dawn 68
40. Bush Fire 69
41. Idle 71
42. The Walk 72
43. On Looking at a Coral Reef 74
44. The Actor's Lament 75
45. Cup of Bitterness 76
46. Five Frigate Firms 77
47. The Moon 78
48. Where I Stood 79
49. The Old Maids and the Bachelor Buttons 80
50. Lamentations 81
51. Manhattan Lullaby 83
52. Innocence 84
53. Look at Me Boy-Chlie 85
54. The Descendants 86
55. The West 87
56. The Slum 88
57. Exit 89
58. The Empty Church 90
59. If I Were 91
60. Hairoun, Hairoun 92
61. On Looking into a Pair of Hazel Eyes ...93
62. To Night 94
63. The Mug 95
64. Last Day, 1980 97
65. Untitled 99
66. Bird of the High Sky 100
67. Drought 102
68. Hairoun Under Sudden Flood 104
69. Hairoun – Genesis 105
70. A Woman of Malicious Wit 106
71. Cricket 107
72. Caught Between Two Titans 108
73. Ask 110

PART A

TIMESCAPE

BY

LANCE BANNISTER

1. SCULPTOR TIME

Look what you've
done to my face:
harrowed its innocence
felled its wild flowers
sowed in their place
experience
sunned with smiles
watered with tears
harvested roses and briars.

You wrinkle my parchment
harden my arteries
vent my spleen
wash my brain

Suns and moons have
measured out my life
and shifting stars
in night's black rosary
counted out my follies.

The few small years
have dwindled into months
the months to hours
the fleeting seconds die
while dew still lingers on the grass.

2. BUS DRIVER TIME
(Bronze 2008)

Telephone poles
out of nowhere
appear and recede
blurring distance
like Ariadne's thread
stringing together milestones
that map the maze
of things remembered.
Your buses huff
and puff their approach
or tiptoe in unseen.
I know not where I've been
or where I go or why
but it seems I've passed
this way before.
I pause, but soldier on
my precious pass firm clutched.
Journeys shorten
fares increase
ride roughens
yet often we rode
to the end of the line.

3. REFINER TIME

Refiner time, lets sing of life and rum
long aged in casks
over-proof that we can spread it farther.
This small gift I ask:
when my cask at last is empty,
our thirst quenched,
my spirit shall run low,
top me up again with Old Brigand
a robust still.
Then through countless aeons
let me sleep
and age, in cosmic store;
that when I wake
I shall be better than before.
O what could sweeter be,
what more divine
Refiner Time,
than drink again
with loyal friends
one more time.

4. SHOPKEEPER TIME

Shopkeeper time you always sell me short.
Weigh out my days in pound parcels.
Fill night's sooty paper bags with big rocks
Tied up with string that looks like it came out of the ark.
When last the four-eye health inspector checked your scale?
And even when your weights are full and overflowing
You don't forget to adulterate.
The stuff in the bag
Always passed its *best used by* date.

As true as John 3:16 "For God so loved the world
That he gave his only begotten son."
I gon report you.
You can put it in your pipe and smoke it.
And you can explain to the inspector
Why even though I paid you up to date,
You still haven't cleaned the slate.
You pick out my future like a pigtail
From the smelly brine barrel that propping up the door.
Holding it with two dirty fingers,
You plank it down, take it or leave it, on the greasy counter,
You welcome every bar-solly you can turn up
From under every stone, to come in the bar,
Make noise and carry on in the worst possible way,
Loud enough to raise the dead.
Let them curse me off because I didn't stand a round of drinks.
Tell me things I never knew about myself
Call me every name except a gentleman.
And you don't on-pick your teet' to stop them
As long as they buying.

The old half empty cobwebbed J & R three-gill bottles of rum
Brekking down the shelf, since Noah was a boy
Labels stained and dropping off
That you shudda` pelt out long ago.
You selling for a pound and a crown:

And you en't paid your license in ages.
The shop door bar up till midday every day.
You never sweep the place.
Flies 'nuff to carr' me 'way.
And you call yourself a shopkeeper?

In fact I gon mek the inspector
Bar up the shop permanently.
But for now bring me a nip of the old bad rum.
Pay you when Friday come.

5. BOGEYMAN TIME

You are the wolf at the door
lion who never sleeps
ghost of our nightmares
"policeman coming for you"
dove cooing
"Moses spoke God's word."
Mother's "Tell yuh fada pun yuh
when he come home."
Fear of the unknown.

6. SCHOOLMASTER TIME
(In memory of my old school-
master Wilkie Cumberbatch)

A lash to my back
a shoulder to cry on,
"constant as the Northern star."
You've scribed your characters
in bold but even hand
upon my yellow page,
punched in my record
through senses, mostly pain,
stored in memory banks
accessed with thoughts
processed in words and deeds.
You've punished my failure
with detentions and floggings
sometimes without cause.
Yet spurred me on
with hope
to gain the winner's circle...

7. OLD BRIDGE PLAYER TIME
(To my father)

You dealt my *bridge*-playing father all the aces,
Long suffering wife, children who tried to please
To sow the seed, bind the sheaves of grass
Work rewarding to the body that sets the mind at ease.
And then you changed the game.

Rubber *bridge* where one rejoiced in a good hand
Against old nemesis was no more.
What mattered now was how well one played the same hand
Against a faceless, business-like brigade of opponents
Whom one had never met and to whom
One had never given cause for offence
Among them *old age, cancer, and their lackeys,*
Intrusion and waste of time.

You robbed him of the days of sober work
The heady days of invention,
As you robbed him of many of his closest friends,
The only solace you left him was *bridge,*

And from the joys of waking, to switching off the last light
Every fruitful hour he plucked and devoured
Worshipping at the shrine *of Bridge*
Hampered only by work and food and calls of nature.
Every moment spent, not in *bridge,*
Was water under the *bridge*, forever lost.
Not even sleep could take away this feast
Sleep, the fallow ground that Nature *bridges*
Between the waking harvests of the game.

He had given up smoking, never used alcohol,
And sexual desire had given him up.
So like Horatio of yesteryear,
He kept the *bridge*
Against all odds *old age, cancer, and their lackeys,*
Intrusion and waste of time.

Four players was full fledged game.
Three, *cut throat*, where all was fair,
Two, *double dummy*,
One, *solitaire.*

The collapsible chair
The shade of the spreading mango tree
The floor, the side of the bed
The hole in the wall
Were but props and scenes and acts
On the stage of *bridge*.
His fellow actors came from every sphere.
There was one charming English white-faced lass
Novice to the game
Who invariably called a spade a club.
And therein lies the rub,
Her Freudian slip was showing
In her ethnic sensitivity
To calling a spade a *spade*.

Ignorance of the game my father could forgive.
He would unveil its mysteries.
'It mattered not whether one won or lost
As long as one played *bridge*.'

Like a good scout, and he was a commissioner in his day
Dads was always prepared
And nothing was more reassuring
Than the feel of a pack of cards in the pocket.
Twisted, eroded, dog-eared, some missing
That time had extracted
His bad teeth rosary.

In hospital when sickness took its toll,
In the middle of the night
When the nurse heard his bell
It tolled not for a bedpan
But for a game of *bridge*.

And in the final days
The sun of well-played hand and the cloud of failure
Peeped through the tangled rigging of intravenous drips,
E.C.G. wires and oxygen mask.
Of the I.C.U. four-masted schooner
With white-stockinged, white-capped, Sister Asgill
At the helm, trimming the jib, lowering the mainsail
Commanding the *bridge*.

The *finesse*, the *squeeze*, the *end game*, the *slam*
Were but cherries in the plate that made *old age*
Cancer and their lackeys, intrusion and waste of time
Easier to swallow as did the sure and certain knowledge
That when the game was over,
Somewhere up there his old bridge-playing partners
Who had made it before him
Had set aside a table for *bridge a*nd for him,
An empty chair.

8. BIRD ON THE WING TIME

You are the bird on the wing
Phoenix, hope reborn
cock that wakes the morn.
Eagle soaring, ruling majestic .
Swan who sings
once before she dies.
Stork bringing life.
Crow presiding
over its demise.
Sometimes ancient,
sometimes dead as the Dodo,

What have I done to deserve this Albatross*
around my neck?
Vulture who pecks my innards without the
 hope of death
harpy who steals my treasures.
Kingfisher, you ride free of space
spurning gravity...
Bat that turns out the light.

*Albatross, bird which when killed brought
 bad luck (From Coleridge's Rime of the
Ancient Mariner}

9. CLOCKS

An *oak and copper* clock that hangs upon the wall
When first wound up goes too fast.
For all too brief a span it carries proper time
But sad to say it doesn't last.
The same express record-breaking clock,
When winding slacks, goes at snail pace.
And so the cycle repeats.
When I question his lack of precision
Reminds, "You got me from the prisons."

A *marble clock* of black with inlaid gold sits upon a bracket
Instead of tick tock like ordinary clocks, boasts, "I can hack it."
She is by nature fast and it is pointless to resist her.
Takes the credit for success with many a filibuster
"If it hadn't been for me you would have missed the bus."
This alpha clock is my mother, my wife
She is the secretary that runs my life
Helps me meet earth-shaking dates,
Fulfill my busy round
Keeps my nose to the grind-stone.

Grandfather clock stands on the floor,
Well grounded, stable, and mature
Like the mills of God grinds slow.
Keeps reminding of what I have missed
Have you forgotten this or that?
Crosses t's dots i's, meticulous
Mundane, pedestrian, useful, dull and flat.

I have a clock that seldom works.
Claims more sick hours than an office clerk
Right now it's on the blink
Medically speaking it has 'a kink'
Can't buy a cup of pepper soup.
Spends more money than it can recoup
In Doctor's examinations blood tests, druggists' bills:
Coughs and colds has countless ills
Horologically speaking, *escapement awry
Pendulum hangs loose not level to the eye.
After many visits to pest control,
It still has termites in the hold.
The old auctioneer volunteered there was something wrong

When, "going once, going twice", knocked it down for a song
At whose lyrics in four letter words I can only hint
For fear of libel I dare not print.
"Keeps perfect time twice a day"
The old auctioneer said, "You can bet on it.
As long as you don't wind it or set it."
*escapement—part of clock that allows pendulum to tick.
A vintage *ormolu of Dresden, proud and regal.
Stands on a pedestal, heir to a long line of majesties
Traces her lineage back to the Czars
Kept their council fought their wars.
"My credentials, 'by appointment to the queen'…
You may be seen but not heard…
On state or civil occasions you will address me
As Your Highness Ansonia, and on bended knee!
I keep right time, to a nanosecond.
If you doubt me, ask my royal patron."
My ormolu uses the right forks,
Moves with the right people
Drops the right names
"If any one asks where you met me",
Tell them *"At Sotheby's"*.

A clock is always striking somewhere in our lives
Giving now worthwhile, now egregious advice
Mr. Fast says "Relax no need to worry."
Mr. Slow says, "You'd better hurry."
When *Mr. Very Slow* tunes his throat
Bet your life you've missed the boat.
The clock is a prism, a mirror
Of one's own experience.
It is you or me.

*ormolu—or…gold, molu …moulded.

10. TIMESCAPE

There's a time to race
and a time to dawdle.
Joshua stopped you
dead in your tracks
with upraised hand.
Inventor of punctuality,
inveterate procrastinator.
"Time", a child cries
and pleads for mercy.
"Time out and life goes on...
shortest in a lover's kiss
longest in penance or
waiting for a pot to boil.
Praised for success
blamed for failure
water off a duck's back.

You measure space
as space measures you
you wear a clock's face
ooze through an hour-glass
minute grains of sand
unforgiving, unforgivable
the rings on the tree
the lines in the face
the missing teeth
the tint of grey
the sculptured rock
the gnarl in the rind
of the evergreen.

You were before Zarathustra
Yahweh or Beelzebub
you are father of Zeus
king of the gods
Chronos himself
child-killer, father of life
unseen, unheard, un-everything
presence inferred.
If you didn't exist.
You'd have been invented.

11. EVENING GARDEN

Sun setting, Venus on the rise
Pomegranate moon hangs low in avocado skies.
Dogs howl
Cats caterwaul
Soukouyans shed their skins
Under the water barrel.
Drowsy evenings fall one by one
Playing back my life in *evening garden.*

Wading through the dog-eared leaves
I paint anew the faded photographs.
Woman-In-The-Boat
Rows 'nostalgia' lane
Each valiant stroke an odyssey.
Cabbage Palms mark
The plodding climb from earth to Heaven
And the plummet back.
Superbo Glorioso flaunts brazen laurels
In my face while Nettles get under my skin
and Shame Lady gives the blush.
Sea grapes recall the heady days, and sparkling time
In fame and vintage racked.

Dead wood shatters under my secateurs
And termites scatter
Like panic stricken refugees in winding droves
Fleeing the cannon's roar
All their worldly possessions slung on cadaverous backs:
And they would brand me
"Meddler, ethnic cleanser…"
But is this a fair charge when it is nature,
Who blue pencils raw celluloid,
deletes, erases , repeats, rephrases,
Providing print copy for sensation tabloids?

Long-leg * gaulin time stalks my gold fish pond
Fraudulently withdrawing bullion
She didn't deposit, citing a brood of hungry nestlings.

*Gaulin –heron

"Wall... and barbed wire fence,
You long have blocked my view
Circumscribed my rights
Trammeled my ways
Divided the 'fertile' from the 'rab'
Who made you arbiter of right and wrong?"

Golden apple on golden apple
Falls athwart the path,
Temptation to instant pleasure
At peril of future happiness:
And so I face the crossroads.

Every tainted scrap that fouls the scene
Invites a buzz of flies, a flotilla of flying paparazzi
Who bring off the scoop, feast and make a mockery
Themselves a feast for spiders' maws
And the lasso of crapaud jaws.
So nature primps and preens her feathers
And keeps her pristine form.

Floribunda Black Rose kisses me
From head to toes.
Yellow Rose behind her arbour
Cloistered, harbours forbidden fruit
While Rose Bud locks her fragrance
Deep enclosed in rooms within rooms
And keeps her nectar prisoner behind petal bars.

Yonder stately Century Palm my twin conjoined
Holds my life and history in her hand.
From first she bound our navel strings
Beneath her roots, baptized with morning showers.
She notarized and catalogued my every deed
Stamped indelibly on her bark.
If as they say she flowers once before she dies,
We'll not fear death while still the flower dagger
That's destined for our heart
Safe sheathed in leafy scabbard lies.

Lignum Vitae's last and sallow leaf
And dry prune-wrinkled fruit
Cast shadows of coming events before me.
Once lusty green, now blighted

Once home for butterfly and yellow breast
Now host for myriad uninvited guests.
They warn, "You too will come to this
Your smooth complexion marred
Your robust trunk once pristine and erect
That steered the Sun, now sadly hung:
No longer life for those you love
The time has come to yield to worthier heir."

Then spoke Gnarled Mahogany
Chieftain of the woody clan
"From earliest days I knew you
A bright and bold young man
When first you rode my branches
And the strength of your right hand
That wielded pods like lances.
You climbed my rugged steeple
Wrote texts on stained glass window pane.
Sheltered in my Gothic arch
From sun and wind and rain.
Now evening comes and brings a ☐omber task.
From which I will not ask reprieve
When I of all my kin
Will bear you to your final resting place
And be your last abode
My erstwhile grey and green transfigured
To the blood red mirror of burnished wood
My branches to chrome-plated handles".

ALL - SEEING EYE

12. PHILOSOPHY

(Debunking the theories of the origins of the universe)

From dawn's translucent white
to inky blots of black star studded night
the search to solve life's beginnings goes on
with none to loose her Gordian knot.

Those who swoon on herb's haunting incense,
on Saturn sated, and flaunting fate,
from shattered dreams, and mangled moons,
their surrealist universe create:

They treasure least the feast of pleasure
drain to dregs the cold dark draught of pain
on sands colossal brand their measure
and laugh at loss as gain.

Nor heed they the Book one mite,
its sage eternal manuscript upstage
for might the finger against them write
they rip the infernal page.

Hal Luci Nogen scrambles the brain
that sees bemused the breeze that blows;
hears the liquor distilled from cane
and swills the hues of rose.

They who from logic's thread suspend
with learning erudite their theories
and with pious pleas their plight defend
under the sword, await the fate of Damocles.

That than which no greater is
must *automatically exist,*
itself is based upon a false premise.
And if it did, what need of casuist.

The *cause of which there is no cause*
propounds a fallacy fatally flawed
for concepts void of facts are vacuous
and lack all earthly proof of God.
Suppose in wild uncharted land

a sophisticated watch you chanced to find
you'd postulate a craftsman's hand
her symmetry designed.

But, *the theory of design* is a suggestion
like infinite regress of hen and egg
which came first? Merely begs the question
or does the question beg?

Science hobbles us with rules
reducing life to laws and molecules.
Within the ambit of her schools
teachers or students, who are the bigger fools?

And still, where herb and logic fail,
can true believer or infidel
by wailing wall or wishing well prevail
to save a soul from hell?

No single faith or sect or schism
commands inalienable right to Heaven.
The colours of the rainbow refracted through a prism
derive from a single source of light.

Earth, fire, wind, water
the elements, through alchemy divine,
alternate their forms of matter
outward and visible signs of mind.

Though different in size, extent and strength,
and varied the form in which they're enclosed,
they share the same properties save wave-length
and the conditions to which they're exposed.

Limitless space, and endless time,
each from each other discrete, defined,
child and mother of matter and mind
ever the twain are entwined.

A drop of water is a microcosm
a grain of sand, a world unborn
a breath of air a spawning protoplasm
a ray a message from a distant morn.

If I should die before my prime
and in green leaf lie interred
who winds my clock, who tells my time,
could He who rang the bell have erred?

If this primaeval earth should falter
dissolve, and melt to water
disembody, totally, vanish, and vaporize,
is it but cosmic waste on timeless skies?

13. KAMAU

Edward
Solomon David Brathwaite
King of kings, blue blood
*Caribbean blue
coursing through your veins
*Edwarde edite regibus
Christophe incarnate, Bolivar
liberator of thought, language
from the fetters of erstwhile masters
and nice new shiny straight jackets;
imposing new order, evolution and
movement, fresh burning Souffriere
killing and enriching.

Baptized in nine-tongue Nile,
amidst the reeds and hyacinths:
hieroglyphs speak for an ageless stylus hand.
His chronicles lie baked in Sumerian
tablets to tell of twisted trails
and entrails bent by battle axe
of bazaars of ivory and men for sale.
You've heard the jungle cry,
seen Kilimanjaro weep.
Reborn in civilization's womb,
did you not kill white fowl for old Pithecanthropus?
Embrace Homo Robustus, meet young Sapiens?
Draw on caves a Ras Akyem theme?
Sifting through the sediment
what pearls, what silks, what perfumes
what painted corals did you bring to Brown's beach?

Kamau, Mau Mau, Kamau
blood brother uhuru
blood flowing, eddying
in the world cardiovascular
where Nile's black artery anastomoses with the white,
as milk with coffee
there they say 'tis most fertile...
There lie silted shards of millennia....

Kamau, Camau, Cammy, Cambridge,
Bridge of Sighs,
'abandon hope all ye who enter here'

but hope burned brightly,
*Pierian spring,
drunk deep.

Brathwaite, Braffit,
Braffits of Mile and Quarter
kip' rum shop, sell salt-fish
lard-oil and bottled sweet water.
Edward Kamau Brathwaite
seed of the diaspora
ferried over the vas deferens of time
settled on Brown's Beach
rooting where the water laps
tapping where fresh water springs
eluding blackbirds' claws and conscience crabs
and the long liquid fingers of the sea,
spreading like a bearded fig tree,
world fertilizing, proselytizing,
nigrating, integrating
spanning thought
sheltering homeless,
ital to the hungry.

Edward Braithwright, Birthright
the world is at its lowest ebb
needs a Mohammed or Christ
a *deus ex machina.*

Come; champion the rights of man,
the rights to which we all are heir,
although Ham's sons
your forbears, O noble scion,
through nature's miserly provision
or careless prejudgment
often lacked the means to self-fulfill,
if not denied outright...
and so must harder strive
to roll the Sisyphean rock
up the intransigent hill ...
Edwardian task...
redress the wrongs with a song.

*Caribbean blue—dark blue in Caribbean sea near the horizon
*Edwarde edite regibus—Edward sprung from kings

*Pierian—pertaining to Pieria, the home of the muses, producers of education and the arts1

14. THE DUMP

A puke of undigested metal
A cult of death
An arena where arms play cricket
With skulls for balls and legs for wicket
A cornucopia of ribs to fashion a concubinage of Eves.
A purgatory where Chaos and I
Wrestle over macerated bodies
And pick their entrails clean
Tearing out their hearts
With undiscriminating talons.
A stadium of steel donkey visage
Chains clanked by the wind
With none to applaud or flee.
A tintinnabulation of odds and ends
A pulpit of silence
A mausoleum of misfits
A serendipity of accidents
This pantheon of the absurd
This Time Machine
That wakes an archaeological Adam
To sift a garbage heap of shards.
This clay that yields only to potters' eyes
And potters' hands the magic glimpse into the divine plan
This quintessence of rust.
This fallen angel dust
This rediscovery of the worthless,
Rehashed by fools
Served up as the ridiculous
To satisfy the undiscriminating.
This dump this eyesore
This breeding ground for mosquitoes and art
This waste
This humbug
This ruin

This dark magic
This dump.

15. T.V.HOLIC

All hail Electron God.
Thy humble servant worships thee
monthly tribute pays thy tax collectors
long mayest thou reign.
Prick multichannel ears
to the talking sky.
Omnipresent stand in every room,
my every need fulfill behind these walls.
Far as the eye can see
I look into thy all-seeing eye
that looks right back at me.
No need have I for sun
my T.V. tan suffices
no need have I of trees with Forest Lawn*.
Snow, a faulty tube provides.
Thanks be to thee
for ladling out my life in sponsors' words…
monitoring my children…
"Child turn down the stove"…
For celluloid 'revolutions'
for cable network 'strikes'
for tabloid demonstrations
for 'right to die'
for soaps
for the C. I. A.
for making my day,
for sharing liberal views though, quote unquote,
"honkies, gooks, and wogs" might disagree…
They say I have an addiction.
Nonsense!
I can kick the habit whenever I want to. Cold turkey!
Uh gone for now. I hear my favourite program coming.

*Forest Lawn –lawn tennis venue.

16. IDENTITY CRISIS

When I was young and white
or so I thought
I often tried to right a knot in my hair
that trespassed on the boundary of my face;
sculpted and refined a nose
by no means aquiline
at mother's importunate prayer
to resemble the fortunate and the fair.
Came the rude awakening
I was coloured
'from rank, and power, and privilege
disenfranchised'
by a lick of the tar-brush.
Then was I 'twenty-four carat' black
and could I trace
beyond the 'middle passage'
a heritage back to roots of Ras Tafari
David's line?
Wrong again,
the black escutcheon was blotted white
the coffee watered down with milk
the proud authentic flare of Africa's nose
eroded by pale Caucasian genes.
"Then, who or what was I?"
a question all might ask
for what black skin
the ebony Ethiop wears
contains no vestige layer of white?
What true blue European blood
closets no black skeleton?
But what before seemed loss
now I deem great gain.

17. PERVERSE GENERATION

I've been accused of
The arrogance of gentility.
(And rightly so.)
Of the impertinence of giving the other man the benefit of the doubt.
(Guilty as charged.)
Of making a misinterpretation favourable to the other side.
(Don't have a leg to stand on.)
Of thinking the other fellow meant well.
(How paranoid can you get?)
Of the utter stupidity of giving way when both sides would have been hurt.
"Soft and spineless!"
Of not carrying arms when I <u>know</u> the other fellow isn't armed.
"No brainer."
Of sticking to the speed limit and letting the other fellow pass.
"Got nowhere to go. You can't drive?"
What a perverse generation!

18. EQUUS

(Erected at the University of Technology at Papine, Jamaica)

I am Equus, hippos, horse.
I spawn the earth and spar the sky.
I am made of iron
And though I come from garbage dump and motor mausoleum
I am the unit of strength, the icon of speed,
The talisman of sexual prowess.

As when Achilles, after years of skulking in his tents,
Beside the walls of Troy, when Patroclus his best friend dies
And his armour is stripped and his body defiled:
Dons <u>new</u> armour and rushes to the fight,
 Like a stallion long pent up...
"He trusting in his strength swiftly his limbs bear him
To the meadows and the pastures of the mares."

I Bucephalus, *Bull-head,* often have I borne Alexander the Great
On my back when he attacked and destroyed mighty empires
And where the Hydaspes laps the shores of India,
In Earth's farthest Eastern sweep
What men now call Pakistan,
I conquered a city and gave it my name.

My *Numidian brethren falling back
And reforming into pincer attacks
Won many of Hannibal's decisive Roman victories,
Trebia, Trasimene, Cannae.

Not all my exploits were as grandiose.
Some have acquired a place in the comic hall of fame.
As when, as Rosinante, Don Quixote on my back,
We tilted at windmills with many a broken lance to prove it
And many a bloody crown to show.

However there were times when we blotted our copybook.
 Pharaoh's Egyptian chariot horses my blood brothers
That had seen the enemy off again and again
Were no match for the Red Sea waves closing in
Protecting the Israelites in their escape from Egypt.

We were famous for our * Parthian shot, a blast of arrows
Fired by our riders over their shoulders in *retreat.*
Snatching victory from defeat.

The Heavens are man's scribbling page.
Here I am, Sagittarius last of the Zodiac, archer on myback
Who writes the year's final chapter in December skies...
I am Pegasus the horse with winged feet
Who took the messengers of the gods
On numberless errands, to star-gazers a child's hobby horse,
To the unimaginative, a rectangle in the sky.

Men call the train the *iron horse* in my honour.
I am the forerunner of the tank.

I *am* made of iron
And though I come from garbage dump and motor mausoleum
My claque see me translated to the skies
Or wrapped in ticker tape preceded by a hundred trombones
Leading the grand parade.

I am no spavined mare or galled-back nag.
That should be put out of its misery, shot, euthanized
Pelted with stones , thrown to the sharks as bait,
Or buried without rites, without words, without gravestone.
To extrapolate from Quintus Horatius Flaccus (Horace)
 "I was erected a monument more lasting than bronze,
I shall not all die."

*Numidia n—from province in North Africa.
*Parthian --shot fired in feigned retreat snatching victory out of the jaws
of defeat.

19. THE TREE

Arms, writhing branches
holding fruits and blackbirds
whose whorled eyes see
harps and ornate worlds
trunk a man
tree roots stand
in diamond sands
beside a ruby sea,
the moon, with her retinue of stars
looks down from topaz sky.
Tree of life and death,
from all eternity
tree from which all trees are planned
tree of man, tree divine
arbor crystalline.

20. VILLAGE

(BARBADOS)

Where blue white waves beat coral pan.
Where palm bush chains the seas with fickle sand.
And black birds sing.
Where the sun is always on the rise.
Where, could we forget,
Gold drove brothers to enslave brothers.
But if the end could justify the means,
Our only hope in this Pandora's box,
That grain of mustard seed has spawned a forest garden
Where class and creed and colour
Live hand in hand.
Where men are free to think,
Express their views loud and clear
In sure and certain confidence,
Their rights embodied in the constitution.
Where little old ladies walk without a care
While grandsons bring unwelcome traffic to a screeching halt.
Where homes have no closed doors
But thieves do not break in.
David, among Goliaths, speaks
And the whole world listens.
This diamond in the crown.
This island that rolls back a sea of tyrannies.
This rock,
Defender of the faith.
This star in the firmament.
This promised land.
This chosen people.
This mother, this father.
This Barbados.

21. BANJOMAN

A mother's prayer was heard, all hell
broke loose, "Lord have mercy, the angel Gabriel,
a miracle, Jesus second coming..."
Or just ole' mass and steel-pan drumming?

For what from far seemed a trumpet's blow
was a lilting guitar and an old banjo...
a son coming home and people by the score
he played and he played, they still called for more.

Corn in its husks from the rafters hung
hermit crabs skittered the white marl floor
the day she heard her long lost son,
tippety-tap at the old half door.

"Boy, Uh so glad to see you.
I bet you *mussy hungry too."
Set him down on the ottoman seat,
gave him all he could drink and eat.

"Morning had cleaned out when I arrived by schooner,
left Shermans, passed Judge Gap, should've got here sooner,
the sun was hot the pace was slow
but quick went the time with the old banjo."

And how they came kith and kin,
from far and near of every skin,
black and white, mulatto and clear,
dark brown light brown, and passing for fair,

Carpenters, masons, slow cantoneers
sugar-cane workers, tanned overseers
fishermen, coopers, peddling their wares,
shoe-makers, barbers, cooks and cane-weighers,

Panamas, bonnets, cork-hats, and bowlers,
peaked caps, lime-skins, white straw-boaters,
hats safely anchored with ivory pins
swishing in scarves of fine muslin,

Dresses billowing down to the toes,
frills, flounces and furbelows,

  petticoats, bloomers, loose chemise,
pinafores waving like flags in the breeze,

Noses, ballroom, flare-nose and fine,
saddle-back, chigger-picker, aquiline;
can't say "prune", but can say "guava",
"shut yuh mout' yuh drink p'ison cassava?"

"Hey nigger-man," chirps a big sister,
"yuh know yuh muddah looking fuh you, mister,
left home since morning to go at the shop,
for half cent in lard-oil... she gon roast yuh chop."

As'ed out, buttons missing, torn at the knee,
cambric, calico , blue dungaree,
they marched, they joked, they wanted to know
where I learnt to play the old banjo so.

"At Walkers estate I went to school,
and there passed out a complete fool...
graduated with honours, Easy Hall, *Featherbed,
won a diploma in 'swinging the lead.'

Playing the banjo to tell you the truth
is only a sign of a misspent youth.
Play the guitar, violjn, sax, or oboe,
but never play the old banjo."

` (*swinging the lead or lead pencil means wasting time)
*mussy—must be....,*Featherbed—actual name of plantation.

22. BARBADOS DAY

Sun, all seeing mother, puts on the pot.
Turns on the light. Her glowing eyeball peeps
Through *Night's* palm shuttered half-door.
Dawn, (who wipes yesterday's slate clean,
Day's youngest child), rises from her watery bed.
Venus' needless candle star flickers out.
Dawn cherry- picks patchwork taffeta of
Candy stick red or buttermilk blue, bright, drab,
Any colour, shade or hue, shedding night's black gown.
Makes wry faces in *Bathsheba's* undulating *Soup Bowl* looking glass.
Conch shell colours *Chalky Mount's* pouting cheeks
Mascara shadows Hackleton Cliffs' overhanging brows
Bathes coral skin in *Codrington's Pierian Spring.*
Flings *Bath Beach* tangled mile-tree hair to the winds.
Cornrows Strong *Hope's* Great House cabbage palms.
Laughs each impish wave that gathers up loose pebbles
From *Cove Bay* rubble, erects Sand Castles
And without a backward glance tears them down again.
Eyes, Graeme Hall lucent mangrove-lidded swamps,
Where *Lordly Heron's* sculpted statue catches fish
And wily *Tarpon's* molting scales
Pave the water paths with silver dollars.

A thousand egrets armed with book-bags, pencils, slates,
Nails clipped, hair combed, shoes polished;
Launch white ships on cloud-capped waves in blue inverted sea.
Doves coo, *"Moses spoke God's word"*
Blackbird from her reedy throat sings of real corn,
Not fools corn dropping from the *Iron Horse.*

Barbados fowl cock, Rufus, from his paling throne
Brings down the house, with his rendition of
"Early to rise," rude awakener, arrogant angel,
Envy of La Scala, with rich contralto, gift of nature rare,
And practised years of scales and midnight oil.
Blood red crown of comb and wattle bib
Buffed breast, gilded wings, neck of azure paint,
Spurs razor sharp, pearl handled nails,
From charcoal black saddle-back cascade
Orange-feather streamers of Vesuvius' lava;
Palette of Ras Akyem or Fielding Babb, whose
Elongated brush and knife, reach down from Heaven's garret

To colour-in Barbados... Sistine Chapel ceiling on the ground.

His backing, treble section of whistling frogs,
Rasping cricket violins, and barking dogs.
On bass, truckloads of slavering toads
Squander beautiful princesses' kisses
With off-key virtuoso bellows organ serenades
And slingshot tongue near-misses.

Bulkeley Sugar Factory boatswain blows the horn.
Trents Plantation overseer rings the mill-yard bell.
Agricultural labourers line up, in time-honoured hierarchy
Flour-bag pants, snot-nose, pond-grass-picking, 'third-class' children's brigade.
Big-bottomed, fat-calved, tie-head, women's gang,
Dress and apron tucked in rolls around the waist,
Armed with hoe-and-basket (tools of trade).
Fork-men leaning on *four-forwards*, ready to change gears,
Copper-banded knife and rice filled calabash on belt,
And under shirt around the waist, cow-skin leather,
Eyeleted, and buckled to canvas as weight-lifting back support.
Salim sahib superintendents *Lord High Executioners*,
*Ocya stick clutched in hand, under crocus-bag 'raincoat',
All ears cocked to hear the orders of the day.

Dawn's land-breeze breathes life into *Morgan Lewis'*
Sugarcane windmill. The ancient galleon's
Canvas sail and greenheart mast huff and wheeze.
Barnacled prow slices the sun into a million minted golden pieces-of-eight,
With each round trip lumbers into port,
Offloading its argosy on the nearby casuarinas.
So money grows on trees. Barbados how blessed indeed!

Noon more buxom and mature stands
Welcoming at *Sunbury Plantation House* front door.
Tables sag under fat-porks, cashews, sea grapes, dunks,
Gleaned in lazy summer time from *Belleplaine Sand Dunes*.
A smorgasbord of juice and fruit, of fallen elderberries,
Foot-crunched, fermented, is steeped in morning dew.
Strained till pure and filled in crystal ewers,
By *Pelican Galleries'* master craftsmen blown and dyed,

.

*ocya—stick used in self-defence

Barbados pride and joy: they lure and cloy and satisfy
We harness *four white horses*, Ben Hur's matching Arabs
To the shafts of *Concorde* buggy, climb the step
To leather button-back seat, gather up reins,
Snap horses' backs, crack whip. Ears prick up.
Ferrule bound wooden-spokes radiating from lignum-vitae knaves
Spin, mortised in fustic fellows, wedged in iron-band wheels,
Race each other, make strobe light blur.
We clatter and dash, Charlton Heston charioteers,
Round the bends, quondam heroes of the silver screen,
Breaking lap records down rutted cartroad tracks,
In sequestered arrowing cane-fields, where honeybee-laden
Pigeon-pea blossoms line hedge-rows, and speckled,
Nine-hand-bunch, bananas, and yellow pawpaws fester
In pond bottoms, and a hummingbird hangs in the air like a pause.

Evening comes, eldest daughter of the setting sun,
Her household chores nearly done, helps late buds unfold,
Gilds green fruit yellow gold, rubs on the sheen,
Softens the core, loosens the seed, matts the shine,
To pass the test of finger-nail, or eye, or nose.
Sugar apple on sugar apple grows old, avocado on avocado,
Enfold in Belleplaine-excursion cabbage-plait baskets.

Evening drives from pasture one hundred contented
Black and white Holstein cows, chewing cuds,
Confines them within metal gates and bre'chin' chains,
White p. v. c. pipes, digital gadgets, in *Morgan Lewis* milking stands:
Floods *PineHill Dairy* stainless-steel milk shipping tanker,
Modern remake of frill-capped, white-apron, milkmaid,
Mary at the garden gate, bucket in hand, scotched
On three-legged stool, milking *Daisy with the crumpled horn*.
Syrup taches overflow. Pan boilers knock off.

Andrews Factory blows steam, sends workers home.
Whistling frogs and crickets strike up the band.
Venus, old lamplighter, lights winged candles,
Evening makes her bed in Western caves beneath the sea.
Brings the end of day, for some and sleep.

We climb lacquered rococo stairs to bedroom.
Crystal bee-hive chandelier hangs from *Paladian ceiling.
Four-poster mahogany bed dominates the room,
Pineapple-embossed legs and Queen Anne headpiece,
Of angel wings and plaited fig-tree leaves,
Promise warm embrace and darling dreams.

While crochet-bordered canopy, draped on carved tester,
Wards off centipedes and arrow-tailed demons of the night.
Cool sweet white sea-island cotton-sheets invite
(Three-generation heirlooms, breathing khus-khus grass perfume,
Ages slept in brassbound chest or cedar lined armoire,
That only wake to honour favoured guest)
Elegantly tossed, or so it seems, on coil-spring mattress,
Herring-bone twined, stuffed with coir and horse hair.

For others *Day* has just begun.

*Paladian—type of architecture

23. BAXTER ROAD AWAKES

Countless streetlight suns rise over rum-shop bar horizons.
Flying-fish land on frying pan runways,
Parked by smoky attendants, spatula in hand,
Faces glowing in the dark, fanning coal-pots.
Corks pop. Stoppers fly. Men prop up bars,
Toss back straight rums. Pan-people beat hell
Outta pinga linga ping pong steel pans.
And *Night* dumps pajamas, wriggles into the little black dress
Squeezes into patent leather dancing shoes
Makes beeline for *After Dark* till ...*Dawn*

24. BAXTER'S ROAD

Baxter's Road is the pale electric sun that rises
by man's fiat when nature's sun has set
dingy worm-eaten bulb of perfume and sweat
that switches on with a glint of silver,
a swish of paper, a jingle of gold.

It is the cathedral of odours, its acolytes sprinkling
dark alleyways with unholy waters and incense of pee.
It is the watering-hole of cons and suckers, bottomless suck well,
hands like buckets winched down begging quarters,
protesting acquaintance of better days,

It is the ear splitting drum of dub
pouring night's libation to morning-after hangover.
The marijuana capital of the world.
Market-place where everything save honour sells,
dock of principles, jury in session,
canvas to the artist, to its residents, home.

It is the campus of the University of Nothing
where bachelors of profanity,
 masters of con,
 doctors of spin
and the graduating dispossessed
make procession in broken dreams
hooded in rags,
gowned in bling bling,
mortar-boarded in sweat
ermined in dirt.

25. BAXTER'S ROAD 2

Baxter's Road perspective
flashes in a paro's smile
miniskirt shadows slanting on sidewalks
paved with fat fish sellers
and human garbage
hubbub of dub, tinkle of glass and beer
titillate the senses numb the sense
and she on whom my life depends
keeps her lonely bed.

26. BAXTER'S ROAD A LA CARTE

Fill the bowl with poetry
generous scoops of Annette Trotman pour
throw in great dollops of Ricky Brewster for body
add Bruce St. John and let the mixture rise.
Season well with Brathwaite
a little Fosta for good measure
with Charmaine's effusions baste
a tang of Gilkes
grind of Mike
beat Tulah drums
sprinkle Gilmore lavishly
crown with coloured rum
cook to a busman Farrell heat.
Baxters Road, eat a bellyful.

27. CRIES OF THE MARKETPLACE

Almanac, Old Moore's Almanac
Baking pans
Ball starch
Baskets
Blind, my lady, the blind
Bottles, got any bottles?
Cane, bundle o'cane, one cent, five pieces for one cent
Cold tar, cold tar
Comfits, toffees or mints, sugar cakes
Corn, shell-corn, who want muh dey
Cow-heel and tripe
Eschallot
Feesh, fre-esh feesh, all a penny!
Ginger
Knives, get your knives ground
Limes , get your useful limes
Mangra*, mangra
Measuring tots,
Milk, fresh milk
Nuts, get your courting nuts
Orangers**
Penny bread
Pomegranates
Rose-tree trimmers*** any rose-trees to trim today
Scissors sharp, get your scissors sharp
Six chances for ten cents (heard on exhibition day)
Skillet of sand
Tea, cooling tea
Travellers (snow cones)
Trimmer, any mules to trim?
Tumbric****
Water, cold water
 What's fat? {speculator with rope looking for fat animals}

*mangra—mango
**Orangers—corruption of oranges
***Rose-tree trimmers—euphemism for toilet scavengers
****Tumbric—colloquial for turmeric

28. RUFUS THE COCK

One fore-day morning
before day cleaned out
a lusty cock-a-doodle-doo
snuffed out my dreams.
From nearby tree it came.
Reveille and a thousand others
blared far and near
re-echoing from every house-top, pen and farm.

There he stood the rude awakener
arrogant angel dressed in morning sun
Cock, a magnificent rooster
from the blood red crown of his comb
and wattled bib of sunset sails
to the tips of his pearl handle nails.
Eye that pierced the thoughts of men
neck of burnished gold and vermeil hues
mocked the sun,
buff his breast and brazen wings
spurs razor sharp.

Pride of Hermes
from graceful saddle back of darker hues
his tail erupted orange streamers.
His rich contralto, gift of nature
envy of a metro talent rare and
practised years of scales
and midnight oil.
All in all a cut above the rest.
He took fortune in his stride,
scion of an ancient line of chanticleers
nature's choice to carry on the race.

Booty foraged,
with one deft stroke of beak and claws
he divided, evenly to the grain,
between his amours
no time himself for mundane food.
They in turn would sweep his yard
comb his hair shower every loving care
beyond the call of duty or desire,
happy to oblige his neighbours' wives himself

though not prepared to share his own.

A handsome stranger passing by
bent on dallying with a fair young maid
thoughtless trespassed his domain
not one of Rufus' wives, the cardinal sin.
To Rufus it was enough,
bore down, transfixed the young Lothario
with his spurs,
raining blood and chastisement
turf defended, honour satisfied.
as befitted his fowl-cock majesty.

29. CIRCE

"Went by Circe last night.
She gimme two white rums and a chicken leg
play some dub, had me horny as hell
went inside, she and she sister
work me over like pros
things you never read 'bout
best night uh ever had
went to sleep
dream and evating how uh was
bathin' down by Batts Rock
how de water warm
and when uh open muh eyes
there uh was
naked as uh born
down in the gutter
purse gone
and a dog wid he hind leg cock
tekking aim like I was a fire hydrant
never me again."

30. COLE'S CAVE

(PERPETUAL SLAVERY)

I Prometheus
From metropolitan exile returned
Freed of the chains of allegory and mindless mantras
Armed with light, slither down earth's gullet
Gripping dread-locked stairs
Hoping to enlighten bat-blind brothers.
Still hanging as I left them
In suspended animation.
Ensconced in cosy crypts
Basking in perpetual night.
They hurled guano epithets
"Lucifer, lackey, sun-eyed Iscariot."
Hoping to dowse Promethean light.
"Let light shine"
Shall these words wash off a duck's back
Or grow stalagmites to the stars?

And in the black- hole of men's minds
The ruthless bird of time
Unravels the tripe of –isms, -ologies, and creeds,
Self-prisoned in the weeping rock,
Deaf to freedom's call,
Blind to other-worldly sight
Unlearned the lessons of stalactites
Timeless scribed in rivers of ink.
And though neo-colonial Bastille
Fall to Bussa's drum
Mind slaves rebuild old wall from rubble.
"Let light shine"
Shall these words wash off a duck's back
Or grow stalagmites to the stars?

31. BUSH DOCTORS

I met a *Weed* a lowly weed,
who soared on wings of family deeds
"You know my daughter, *Holly Hock*" she volunteered,
"She's done her doctorate on medicinal milk.
Its cleansing action on the skin.
Cassia Stinking Toe her next of kin
makes house calls
black bag, sugar coated pills and all.
Physic Nut Berry and *Clammy Cherry*
keep chemist shop, steeping cooling teas
for ills real and imaginary.
Seed Under Leaf *(Grenbafwi),
stimulates the brain,
while Grenbafwi's last boy *Gully Root*
specializes in back street abortions"
went her sweet refrain.
"Auntie *Cerasee* is 'Cure-For-All'."
She prattled on, while hoary *Whitehead Bush*,
Her sister's cousin's aunt held his ground
signing autographs on my new
Sunday-go-to-meeting designer serge pants.
"All hail illustrious knight of the galley,
scion of an ancient line of scullions
third generation Lord High Panjandrum
scourer of pots and pans and ottomans:
high priest of every service-o-song
minister's lackey, and arse licker,"
I hailed him.
Cactus halberdiers, *Weed's* knights-at-arms
and *Gru Gru* palm musketeers crossed blades
to foil my 'clear intention'
of 'overthrowing their government
and reversing the revolution'.
But *Rising Sun* snuffed out
the *Jack-O-Lanterns*
and nipped it in the bud.

*grenbafwi—*grain bas feuille* , grain under leaf

32. SATURDAY NIGHT

At a loose end
in need of a friend
phoned Sue
she had the flu
rang Kate
she had a date
went by May
strange car in driveway
on my route
you were out
gone to church.
In the lurch.
thought 'bout Allyson
what I was missin'
name in the book
phone off the hook
remembered Vicky
too darn picky
tried Grace
"out de place".
Why not Mignon
back in England.
Can't ask Pat
"done wid dat"
finally, "Joanie's phone
leave your message at the tone..."
Wha' happen wid me,
I got leprosy?

33. BRITTONS HILL CAVE-IN

Of rocks and beams and twisted metal
And chasms and screams and echoes and silence
And blood and flesh and broken teeth
As though a schizophrenic father-earth
Had flagellated himself
And saved his wife and children from a life of pain
Only to execute them and himself in his final 'solution'.
"I bring them in this world, I feed them,
 I kill them."

Of old Chronos throwing his son Hephaestus out of the crib.
And sending serpents to kill baby Hercules.
Of the lion, new heir to the throne of king of beasts
Killing his pride's cubs who are not his own
To wipe the slate clean and guarantee his own D.N.A.
Of an Oedipus father who threw away the script,
That said that he should die, at the hands of his son
Who turned the tables and killed his son.
Of an unfortunate Abraham
Who found no *ram caught in a thicket*
And sacrificed Isaac his only son.

Of bones and blood and sinews dripping from
Giant Polyphemus overfull man-eating mouth.
And Odysseus and his men
Catered as the giant's last supper.
Of skeleton and flesh quarrelling and deciding to part.
Of wars of the elements earth, wind, water, fire
Of apocalyptic preview of the end of the world.
Of lymphocytes and corpuscles when life has gone out of the body
Salvaging anything that is left trying to resurrect life.
Of Martin Luther King who had a dream
And Barack Obama and *all the king's men* who had the *audacity*
To hope to put Humpty Dumpty's world together again.
Of a sick earth that cures itself by suicide.
Of rocks and beams and twisted metal
And chasms and screams and echoes and silence
I weep.

34. MOONLIGHT AND MORNING

Gas lamp highlights deserted street.
Long neglected door creaks half open on unused hinges
Like smile of sweet surprise from faintly parted lips.
Firefly flashback changes night to day all too brief.
Twisted staircase, till now forgot, leads the way to her boudoir.
Morning star shatters heavenly dreams, all too real.
The cock-a-doodle-doos, with promises of worms and love.
Sun opens Caribbean-blue eyes on white silk cotton skies.
'The hunter of the East' lassoes 'rosy fingered dawn';
And polished bronze or mercury mirror
Cannot compete beside the shine of wet October canes.
Model T Ford backfires and raises blackbirds' hopes for undigested corn.
Donkey's bray counts hours for mealtimes and meditation.
First shimmer of hot roads builds Sam's Castles in the air.
The taste of sugar crystallized in ancient windmill
Blends with smell of bitter almonds.
 So sweet and bitter marry in glucopicric harmony.
Venus rises from her bed, scatters perfume and desire
Haunting wistful fragrance clings to my coat and scarf.
The simple rustic scent of mignonette pervades her yard
The tongue-twisting, gland wrenching salivation
Of flying fish fried to her perfection while I wait
But dare not touch till the table is laid, and the bell rung.
Red stained feet crunch evergreen berries, while branches laden
With yellow ripened guavas threaten to crash into the head.
A diva in a khus khus *Scala* sings "Brown girl in the ling";
Frogs croak in ponds of lotus and lilies.
Odours of saltfish and pigtail barrel under the counter, curl upwards.
Paddle sloshes buttermilk in earth-ware churn, and the tide is in.
Yellow flagged maypole floats preside at a catching-sea-egg party.
The look in her eye that says it all.

35. SPEIGHTSTOWN 1

(THE LETTER)

I still recall the letter
with many a postmark
and "Try this address"
that brought me
ecstasy
and took it all away
and this is what it had to say.
"My love,
it's you I dream
and old Speightstown, its narrow roads
and balconies of yesteryear
Gothic stained glass cathedral
and needle spire
that pricks the bubble of material things:
choir that sings eternal love
brass bound lectern perched on eagle's wings
lesson taken from the epistle to my heart
voice of conch shell song
and moses catching quick silver
along a barnacled jetty
sooty soup kitchen ---
 rickety theatre
kiss of dark perfume
voyage on the '*Riptide'
the promise that we'd never part
while one solitary sand grain clings to the shore.
Your own sweetheart
Nella."

And on the yellowed envelope
below the sender's address
a handful of black tears had etched
"Nella King is dead."
Nella,
 the night winds shriek,
on cobbled streets
in old Speightstown.

*Riptide—famous Speightstown fishing boat used for racing.

36. SPEIGHTSTOWN 2

(The Old Fishing Village)

The other day, I dusted off a snapshot
tucked away in childhood memories.
Your face as young as now, Speightstown
timeless jewel set in narrow ways
balconies overhanging long lost yesterdays
reach out and stay the passing foot of time.
A gothic chapel pendant on your brow
with stained glass windows and picong spire
pricks the bubble of material things
and man's desire. And in the air
the conch shell sings, "Flyin' fish all-a-penny"
and boats offload their catch on barnacled jetty.
And sooty soup kitchens sell souse and black pudding.
Speightstown vernacular against your lips is pressed
and 'Riptide' fishing-boat rises and falls in the haven of your breast.
"No I will never change," you say
"though the sea rearrange my shore"
your voice frozen in a shutter click:
and my thoughts drift back to the now.

PART B

POETRY AS COMPANY

BY

MARCIA HAROLD HINDS

37. EVENING THEMES

Evening (1)
Evening slid into place
As a cooler breeze began to race
Toward the setting sun
And I said grace
As I'd always done
For the sinking beauty
Of the orbed one

Evening (2)
Evening slid into place
Like a lady in lavender lace
Flirting with some wisps of it
By letting the breeze displace
And veil it
Across her pretty face

Evening (3)
It was one of those evenings
When luminescent lilac light
Heightened the blush
As if applied by a painter's brush.
Except in one conspicuous corner
Where ragged altocumulus cloud cover
Looked like nothing so much
As if cats with dirty paws
Had walked across the canvas
And I thought:
There should be laws.

Evening (4)
The orb approaching sunset
Hung above the horizon
White
Without light
White against a featureless white sky.
You could stare and stare
For it was far from bright
Just
White.
Pale.
Pallid-pale

Ashen even
Without luminescence.
Like a veiled moon.
Just white.

Evening (5)
I noticed it first from the kitchen sink.
My neighbour's house was glowing gold.
Gaping and trying not to blink
I ran into the open to be embraced by the bold
Of an all-encompassing sunset glow.
It was one of those sunsets, you know them,
Where light with ebullient splendour
Escapes sky boundaries to bind the earth in tandem
So that instead of looking up to beauty rendered
We were all awash in beauty tendered.

38. I WRITE NOT BITTER BITING RHYME

I write not bitter biting rhyme
Of social ills and human crime
Nor yet of ever-vaulting passion
And all-consuming vanquishing ambition

These wield power, emotion, action
That stir hearts and minds to a sort of satisfaction
Their language replete with imagery and spleen
That enrage for a future, justified but still unseen

They roar at us with anger, impatiently pawing ground
Till we do trumpet after them, sound upon sound
Or surge forth enwaved beating with our flukes
Justifying most mightily applause or rebukes

But calm follows always the storm
When so tranquil the depths of the forest
So serene the mid-ocean form
And peace, perfect peace, enfolds us once more.

Then is there moment, time, and place
Quiet calm, descending grace
When someone must look out and see
The beauty of a bumble bee

Someone has to turn an eye on to the jewelled hummer*
Someone has to draw you to the loving warmth of summer
Someone has to hold you near a sweet scented flower
Someone must remember the haunting tale of the ruined tower.

Someone needs to show you, you must hold your breath in
To hear leaves rustle, and music in the river water's din
Someone must gentle your hand on a fragile butterfly's wing
And tune you in when blackbirds sing

Someone must walk with you and feel you quiver
As you bathe fully in the moon's soft silver.
That's why I do not write bitter biting rhyme.
There are other themes in place and time.

 * the humming bird

39. DEW AT DAWN

I sat and watched
The jewels of the dawn
Carelessly scattered at my feet
On the lawn.
With heresy, I thought,
I thought.
They're so bright
You'd think man had wrought
Them to create
Scintillating
          Kaleidoscopic
                    Titillation
Mesmerizing
          Hypnotic
                    Concentration

For these water jewels are
No less brilliant than polished stone
But transient
     Transmutable
               Ephemeral
A passing carnival that sun alone
Can gloss so carelessly.
Their beauty lies in distance
And dies if perchance
You touch them.
Yet every morning they can reappear
In some green patch
That's somewhere near
Transparently transmitting joy
That's far from transient
And cannot cloy.
Dew are gems of the dawn
Spread casually across my lawn.

40. BUSH FIRE

Sudden veiling of the view
In drifts of hazing blue
Proclaim a fire somewhere
Devouring bush
In sweeping tongues of flame.
Some place near.
Yes! Here comes scorching fire's flare
Leaping in pursuit of the racing wind.
Blazing, razing, roaring
Hotly chorusing
Through the afternoon air.

Amid the grass and weeds
So many trees stand timber-dry
And bare their woody branches
In skyward supplication
Unable to escape the raging conflagration
Trapped in stolid immobility
Encoded in genetic secrecy.
In a moment they are ablaze
In heated ardour
Aglow in fiery blooms.
Living, leaping,
Crackling, cackling,
Hissing, blistering,
Roaring and scorching.
An awesome sight of
Glorious splendour.

But even as flame earth-rivals the sun
The wind atop the fire
Contains the reality to come
In the heavy burden of
Feather-light black ash
That dims the face of the sun.
There is grace
In the swirling ballet of the ash
As it alights and lifts
And drifts and shifts
Pirouetting repeatedly.

The show closed.

The blackened world was then exposed.
Seemingly, the earth inherits
Nought but scorched earth
And standing skeletons.
Nothing crackling, nothing leaping
Nothing blazing, not a thing glowing
Except hope
That the rains would come
And bid sweet hidden life
Come forth again.

41. IDLE

The afternoon is washed
With sunshine
Making mood
Seem soft and white.
Boys in a distant schoolyard
Play football.
A line of youth make their way
Along a narrow path
Above a cliff
Homeward from the beach
Their laughter light and carefree.
Birds peck at the lawn
Flit in trees
And arc in the air.
One man trails a cow.
Both silent.
I am idle
And as silent.

42. THE WALK

Eagerly I walk towards the promise
Of the rising sun
Keen to exercise my body into shape
But I soon stand still to laugh at the audacity
Of two defiant stars
Peeping round the edge of the paling
To see Sky change into blue dress
And pink scarves for morning vespers

I pause again to grin at birds
Out for the early worm
And wonder where the flying bats call home
I look up with admiration deep to see
How the trees dispose
Their varied limbs and leaves
In fine art entitled
"Green on Blue"

I smile happily at every flower
Of every weed. I stop by them
For everyone is beautiful
From a distance the dew on grass
Reminds of frost that once affrighted me
In not so temperate lands
But up close each sparkling jewel
Brings forth a delighted chuckle

I return from my walk with
The risen sun to back of me
And pesky insects take the
Casual way I brush them from my face
As a greeting. Jain-like I desire
To kill no ant and hope every frog
Has found his favourite hard blanket
To snuggle under for the day's long sleep

I've been walking several weeks now
And no I have not lost a kilogram
But every morning
Nature stretches my imagination
And tones up my mood

And the muscles that make me smile
Are well-exercised indeed.

43. ON LOOKING AT A CORAL REEF
(BARBADOS)

Said one coral to another
(Not foraminefera)
This is a goodly work we do
To be an heritage unsurpassed.
This monument to our culture
Will last and last and last

A shark overhearing, said to a baracuda
I don't know about last and last
Here we compete with bass and snapper
Living one day at a time
Searching for breakfast, lunch and dinner
For as surely as I can see you none is here for ever
So where's the sense in what they do
Building for a future?

But one brainy coral said to another
Standing near one like a stag at bay:
Build, good brother, build away
For we never know when the acts we do
Live after us.
Come! Master your reflexes
Much good is oft interred
In our skeleton complexes
And after years of being buried
Become the means of monumental dreams
For we may suffer a land change
Into something rich and strange

44. THE ACTOR'S LAMENT

What part did I play
At Calvary that day?
Same as now is all I say
Hypocrite, glutton, liar, blasphemer ...
Just ask the redeemer
For I was there in all these roles
Please!
Ask not for whom the bell tolls

45. CUP OF BITTERNESS

I was drinking grapefruit juice
When I heard the news
Bitterness then rasped my tongue
And iciness shocked my teeth

Brothers, sisters
Cousins, uncles
Converged for last respects
And final rites for mother

Must follow the cortege
Must follow
My wife in funeral black
When a white van blind-sided

Now I, the widower
Sit before a window framing nothing
"Eat something'
A sister said

Take this draught
The doctor said
'Drink something'
A friend said

Bring me juice, I said
Grapefruit

46. FIVE FRIGATE BIRDS

(This piece was written to commemorate a most unusual visitation by these birds over my house in Barbados. They were never seen before or after this visit)

Where did you come from?
What a splendid span of wings!
Five pairs in perfect harmony
In unflappable unity
Five acting as one

Hover, hover, wheel and turn
Grace personified
You came in on my right
And I recognized you on sight
Close to midmorning 'gainst a cloudy sky

High up in the air
You hovered o'er my house
Angled wings outstretched
And joy knew no bounds in me
For a visit so unusual

Black wings widespread
White necks exposed
I felt the blessings poured on me
For full half hour
Before with one mind

And a truly casual grace
You rode a current
Slowly eastward.
From where did you come?
Where did you go?

47. THE MOON

I rose dispiritedly from my bed
And walked across the room
I lifted lack-lustre eyes ahead
And saw the moon
It rose above the trees it lit
Defying some dark cloud
Which later deeply hid it
But to whose dark shroud
It gave a silver lining
As I watched this game of skyway tag
My lonely burden lifted
For if despair is like a cloud
As we so often say
If you look closely
You will see
A brightening gleam of
New opportunity

48. WHERE I STOOD

I saw two lonely birds
Fly past the morning moon
And rows of hovering clouds that soon
Seemed stalled o'er a tranquil sea
The sky was blue
The sea a deeper hue
As I stood alone with the rising wind
To east of me

The sun broke the horizon
To selectively stroke with light
And begin the dispersal of night
Setting this aglow but not that.
Peace was sublime
In this morning moment time
And poured a timeless benediction
Over me

For as morning walked
Across earth's turning face
My brain with pride began to race
For some deep cosmic thought
Something philosophic
Something Philistinic
But I was muted and blessed just
Where I stood.

49. THE OLD MAIDS AND THE BACHELOR
BUTTONS*

Side by side in the old garden bed
Stalked old maids white and chaste
Side by side where the garden walk lead
Maids were in mauve and circumspect taste
Between them both, and before and behind
Stood bachelor button taking pride
In their stiff-necked little heads entirely resigned
To bachelorhood until the day they dried.

The bachelors did nod stiffly when a cool breeze blew
And the old maids fluttered when butterflies flew
Yes, all the mauve bachelors, and the white ones too
Starchily bowed an old-fashioned how-de-do
But the old maids privately thought them a pain
Even as they delicately spread their skirts
Making curtsies to them in the light summer rain
They were thinking: They just suit damned stuffed shirts!

*Flowers that are common in gardens in St. Vincent

50. LAMENTATIONS
(This piece is taken from a work of the author called "Ciprian Rejoice".written to commemorate the 100th birthday of St. Ciprian's Church, Belleville, Barbados

Storm tossed am I
Flotsam and jetsam
Powerless am I
Noisome and tiresome.
Drifted, sifted,
Billowed through time's ocean.
Flung down, lifted
Tossing and bashing were my portion
Below the decked stage
Now rifled, stifled
Outcast of the age.

My God! My God! Why have you forsaken me!
Have you forsaken me?

Beaten, bruised and barred
From the altar to God who loves
Battered, burned, charred
Altar-gift to He who gives?
Oh! What an orphan am I!
From signposts of ancient piety
Have I not sought you by and by
In ages past, O Deity?
Am I not child who attended grove
In vault of cathedral trees?
And raided my hands while birds did rove
As I praised on bended knee?

My God! My God! Why have you forsaken me?
Have you forsaken me?

Are you not still the God of Obe?
Are you not still Yahweh to Sara?
Are you not still Allah to Kinte?
Are you not still Jehovah to Leah?
Krishna, hare Krishna, to thee
I voiced my call to reach like Buddha
The narrow Tao that leads us free
From the Babylon of I-man Jah

Babel! Babel!Your thunder crash
With vision-taking dust has
Muted all our stubborn ears
And moted all our eyes.

My God! My God! Why have you forsaken me!
Have you forsaken me?

51. MANHATTAN LULLABY

(This one was actually written in New York City. It is a counterpoint to the rural and other naturalistic themes prepared for infants to this day. My infant children were with me).

See how the bright-lit panes of glass
Pattern the walls of the concrete pass
See how the mighty stacks of light
Paint the canvass of the night

Look up, look down, look all around
Were you to count you'd never get done
And your eyes already blink about
Like two little lights that are winking out

Lie down my little urban child
Cocooned so high above the wild
Dream that every single glow
Is from some urban angel's halo
Sleep little urban child, sleep
Hosts of city angels keep you.
Sleep.

52. INNOCENCE

Nothing is more innocent
Than a child in a deep deep sleep
Little smiles play about the lips
If into the mouth no thumb slips
All is quiet when baby's at rest
Lifting only the lace upon her chest
All is quiet, for the earth mutes her sounds
To marvel that such perfection abounds.

53. LOOK AT ME BOY-CHILE

You look real nice
Dress down in pyjama fuh bed
An' it look like me little brown spice
Goin' be fas' asleep in a trice

Look at me boy-chile
Cute fuh so
Come on! Flash me that smile
Boy, you're the sweetes' chile

I love that grin
You is one han'some boy!
But Mr.Sleep is sitting pon your chin
He, or he identical twin

Look at me boy-chile
Cute fuh so
Come on! Flash me that smile
 Boy, you're the sweetes' chile

Sleep sound, me son
While I watch over you
Is play I play with you till de day done
Come tomorrow, there'll be much more fun.

Look at me boy-chile,
Cute fuh so
Come on! Flash me that smile
Boy, you are the sweetes' chile

54. THE DESCENDANTS

Folk still plant
According to their tears
And irrigate the waving green
With sweat.

Folk still ratoon
With habit down the years
Where the harvest lightening-lash
Synchronizes thundering sighs.

The field is cane.

55. THE WEST

In the west
Africa bridged
The European chasm
And with voodoo
Tangoed with their hoodoo
Inextricably.

In the west
Africa and India
At last collided
And served up coocoo
With blends of curried
Spices.

In the west
AfricaAsiaEurope
Merged back into the
Wholesomeness
Of creation
And restarted a vital sign.

56. THE SLUM

Not yet thirty
Hardened as fifty
Mothers watch
Pot-bellied children
and the pot
Boil meatless fare
A foot or two
From the gutter
Where the city's waste
collects
and is collected not.

57. EXIT

I saw a frog
Ready to pass on genes
Seek water

I saw a bird
Hunting a nesting site
Seek leaves.

I saw a butterfly
Pining for nectar
Seek blooms

I saw a dust-grimed farmer
With water only on his beard
Face the empty road.

58. THE EMPTY CHURCH

We raised the walls
We laid the floor
We spanned the roof
Glass filtered colour
Except
The Light of the World

Jewelled vestments fluted
The organ piped
But no sound reflected
The still small voice
Of
The Enlightening Word

Styles high as heels
And heels like Pharisees
Looked straight ahead
And never saw a soul
Nor
Eden's hovering sword

God's voice called over the void
Echoing through the vaulted dome
And Jesus wept:
You do not see the hurting heart
Your head is turned aside
And only rite is right.

Habit does not make a nun
Anymore
Than a habitation
God's house.

59. IF I WERE ...

If I were beautiful
I would be good

If I were strong
I would be fair

If I were rich
I'd fix the world

If I had power
I'd empower the weak.

"If you had these
You would norm
To those that have them."

Who says?

'Perhaps
The God of your present.
Do not hold your goodness
Servant to what is really
Wished-for grandeur.
Do not predicate life on 'if'.
What you can do now
Is good enough.

If...?

If is a preposition
Not a proposition.

60. HAIROUN, HAIROUN*

Where
Green mountains dominate
Rough-edging the doming blue
And rain-sodden clouds roll by and mate
Fecund soil with fallen dew

Where
Lullaby rhythms time the swells
That roll along and break
O'er bone of my bone which sleeping dwells
To be spewed forth in the last Great Wake.

Where
Rivers play orchestra
With flute and rattle
Xylophones and drum.
Jubilating to the sea
Hairoun is Me.

Bound by the sea
Hairoun is me.

* Hairoun has been traditionally one of the indigenous Carib
names for St. Vincent and the Grenadines

61. ON LOOKING INTO A PAIR OF HAZEL EYES

Limpid pools
Flirting through curling reeds
To caress and play
With light and shadow
In subtle tones of
Brown and green
And smouldering embers
Of truest amber.
I wish to dive into
Such golden loveliness
And drown in gay abandon!

Ouch! I'd better not say that!
What a pity.
It is so apt.

62. TO NIGHT

The yellow sun
Its course has run
Day is done
Night to summon
On wings of falcon
And swiftly silently
Sun slips beneath the sea
Without green flash
Before the dark sets free
The winking stars eagerly

This changing of the guard
From daylight to night's ward
Did pay full regard
To ceremony. Colour came hard
Upon colour as the charred
Velvet of the night
Bestrode the twilight
With its own delight
For every star was a sprite
Twinkling into sight

Night is not day's
Step-sister; no tears
Need be shed and no fears
Held as to how she pays
Her worldly way. Here's
A coquette knows winsomely
The lasting value of mystery
The mystique of secrecy
The haunting allure of veiled beauty
Of promise dark and heady

63. THE MUG

**(The inspiration for "The Mug' is a composite of people
and the way they cling to ordinary articles in memory of a
loved one. It also says something about the stages of man).**

There it sits in the corner of the cupboard
No one uses it now, this slim
Plain mug in an ordinary green
Topped with a deep-brown rim
No pattern anywhere seen

It gathers dust I will admit
Though it's washed when we spring clean
At the lip is a little chip
And on the handle a crack is seen
But still sturdy from hand to lip

This mug marked a chequered life
Its first years hot with the aroma of coffee
Then abruptly without explanation
It steadily steamed with tea
Till cocoa hallmarked relaxation

Those action-filled years to achieve
On the move with frenetic fervour
It was coffee on the run
Make it sweet make it strong
Work! It never seemed done!

Then came days that moved more slowly
The ones reflected in tea
With much talk effusively
Of the changing days and the change in ways
The years of philosophy

Too soon, the wrinkled face to the cocoa bent
As the pace of life stood still
The restlessness now for others
He sat with his mug by the windowsill
Observing the antics of youngsters

My grandfather's mug. For so many years
He used it through thick and thin

And no crack ever seemed to impair
Whatever hot drink was within
A souvenir of his life and career

Many are the years since grandfather passed
From this world on to his rest
And we took the mug and placed it
Where we could see it best
In a glass cupboard to encase it

We remember the hands that held it
The flare of his nose with the fragrance
Before savouring the beverage within
This mug is a source of remembrance
Where so many fond memories begin

64. LAST DAY, 1980

(This one is one of my existential experiences. How my thoughts followed a lone rich man in the midst of fun. The scene was New Year's Eve at one of the world's most exclusive hotels).

Crowded table ahead
Jewel-bedecked necks
Of a colour that said
Sun caressed on open decks

He sat alone

Smiling group behind;
A rhinestone cowboy
Texan designed (?)
With a breastless toy

He sat alone

Reminiscent of a Greek
Like an Onassis
Over seventy not meek
But I observed his crisis

For he sat alone

Reverential waiters hovered
He ate lobster, quail and fruit
Deferential servers uncovered
Each dish of his choice acute

But he sat alone

Merry laughter swirled
Discreet though it was
Pampered ladies twirled
Simpering for cameras

He sat alone

Later on I glimpsed him
Sitting solo at the edge

Of laughter's whim
As on a forgotten ledge

He sat alone

The new year came in
And he rose while
Gaiety made din
And on impulse I smiled

At him alone

The faintest smile
It came and went
No guile
The moment was spent

He walked on alone

Did he see my smile?
Did life flare a moment
Or did my fancy overide me while
Facing a lonely torment?

For he was always alone

Over is the evening with its favours
The bright festoons
And ever-ready noise makers
The bursting balloons

Is history

Did anyone wish him joy of the year?
Did anyone at any time
Lighten his rich despair?
Did any see behind his pantomime

As he sat alone?

I now can only atone
With a prayer that God go with you
Man who sat alone

65. UNTITLED

I walked beside a poem
Which babbled like a brook
With a rush of words here
And a plunging phrase there
And a soothing sibilant
Stillness nowhere.
Everywhere it sprung a thought
Giving order to nought
But numbing the mind for a spell
It was like descent into a kind of hell.
Then it made a helicoidal twist
Spiralling to list
With playful vowels
Bound by tight-fisted consonants
That made the poem flow out and on
And stay and leave upon
The mind some image bright.
For the poem made light
Of everything around
While I stalked earth-bound.

The earth speaks in poetry
With little sophistry
We try to reproduce its beauty
With rhyme and metre and symmetry.
But sometimes so rich a fare
Although we dare
Speeds beyond our words' capacity.

The poetry of earth is never dead
Some may just have to be left
Untitled and unread.

66. BIRD OF THE HIGH SKY

Black is so beautiful in you
Wonderful bird of the high sky
Up where you nest against the blue
And rest the weary eye

Your hypnotic act gives pleasure
For my eye seems not to stray
From your seeming act of leisure
Which you provide each day

How truly beautiful you are
How mesmerizing to the eye
Beauty framed in picture stillness
Against the midday sky

Artful perfection of ideal shape
In double-angled wings of elegance
Outstretched, they seem to drape
And bless my every glance

Fluidity of motion in syncopation
Aerodynamic flow's in stillness
You hover without thought of duration
Shrugging gravity as silliness

Yours is melody of motion
No hurried jerky flapping
You do a graceful glide o'er ocean
No flurried wings a-clapping

But the idleness is illusory
Isn't it? For you eye the cobalt ocean
For fish to feed your nursery
Where they await their portion

So many quiet pleasures here
In the flight of the frigate bird
For me, just seeing you in the air
Is balm for this world absurd

Wonderful bird of the clear high sky
Never depart the coast of Hairoun

Beautiful bird of the soaring high sky
Your enchantment I'll seek again soon

67. DROUGHT

The mind was as dry
As the parched earth
Which for weeks had received
Not a sip of quenching rain
Past mid-May
And all remained as proclaimed
By holiday-touting brochures.
Bright puffy clouds
Just touched blue canopy
And sea sand glistened
A blinding white
And made the sea in shallow pools
Appear the only thing cool.
Poui and frangipani
Seemed careless of the gift withheld
And rioted with colour.

The days were hot and airless
And life was
Sunday-midday still
In sight and sound
As if siesta were desired.
Mahogany, flamboyant
And golden-apple
Were skeletons
But the shak-shak had dressed itself
In chattering pods
Shattering the quiet with gossip
Whenever breeze obliged.
Not much.

A bird called
Loud and clear
And for a moment stirred
The quiet air.
Shrugging
I closed my eyes
For my empty brain
sought no relief
Desired no quenching
Just settled down to sleep

And united
With the silence.

68. HAIROUN UNDER SUDDEN FLOOD

Helter-skelter through the rain
See school children run in vain
Pitter, patter, pitter, patter
Raindrops drum with horses' hoofs
Pitter, patter, pitter, patter
Cussing down the galvanized roofs.
The slanting grey sheets hit the ground
And gather and surge with increasing sound
In a mad roll through swollen gutters
Then spill their muddy guts with raucous mutters
On to fields and into yards, lapping
At doorsteps and sapping
At supports with mean intent
As water rushes hell-bent
Brown and boiling
Roiling, toiling
Stampeding with rage to merge with rivers
Brown and soiling
Twisting, coiling
Foiling effort to disentrain debris
Caught in the mad rush to the sea.

Hairoun
Under sudden flood.

69. HAIROUN – GENESIS

You with the myriad mountain slopes
Which you yourself upthrust
From fiery cauldrons
Buried in the depths of earth
When you vent your version
Of the Big Bang
In a fiery passion.
The craters that cradled your creation
Have mellowed serenely
In Marriaqua, and Villa and Kingstown.
Leaving La Soufriere to serve as reminder
That though emerald waters lie
Still as deep thought
You do but sleep.
 (1971 before the last eruptions)

Ah! You have twice rumbled
Grumbling out some
Internal dissatisfaction
You wanted righted.
Do it.
But pray
Easy, girl, easy.
Try using more loving technique
And less passion.

70. A WOMAN OF MALICIOUS WIT

She was a woman of unbridled wit
A woman of malevolently
Malicious wit
She knew a bit
Of everybody's secret business
And contorted it
And tortured it
Until it fir
Within her spiteful wit
And then she spilt it
Heavy laden she spit it
Bit by injudicious bit
In the order that her wicked wit
Had so distorted it.

She was a woman of vindictive wit
On her doorstep she would sit
And whip the frothy gossip
From her lip
Beating it into a maelstrom
With every dip
Everyone cringed and clutched their bosom
Hoping this was not the time she would strip
And flagellate them

Until someone said
'We keep this bitch in business
If we give her no audience
She will lack all credence
And consume her sick self.'
Not a whit too soon
They slipped from her company
For once you get to know it
A nasty twit is
A nothing twit
And this woman of malicious wit
Met her match
And quit.

71. CRICKET

The cricket we played in our yard
With coconut bat and lime for ball
Would make today's players cry hard
But on it we grew strong and tall

It had rules, ours, not theirs
One man to bat at a time
Seldom we batted in pairs
And all fielded the ball

If the lime wasn't found upon fielding
But was lost in the hedge or the drain
Then the lime tree on hand was still yielding
And the game put under no strain

Each man was his own team of one
And batted until he was out
Clean-bowled or caught and you're gone
Any other call was a fight and a shout

As for making runs in this game
Unknown were quotas or ceilings
...Thirty-six, thirty-seven ... panting and lame
You stopped yourself without umpire appealing

Thus losing the ball was like money in the bank
You put as much as you could on deposit
Not hard to do let's be frank
For the lime was as green as the leaves that hid it

In cricket season we played from morning till night
Everyone a Valentine or Ramadin
Lunch and tea breaks were to settle any fight
So you could imagine the din

O what a glorious time it was back then
In the land of galloping youth
Where has it gone?
Which way and when?
Tell me, tell me truth

72. CAUGHT BETWEEN TWO TITANS

I am born to maritime shores
And island seas of precious rocks
In liquid metal
Each rock a gem
A jewel of finest carat
Crafted in hues of infinite grade
That colour an incredible arc
Across the neck of siamese tatans
Which when they storm
Disturb the ripple of ruffles
That lace the breathing cobalt ocean.
Here am I
Drugged with odour from one side
Caught in the stench of superpower
Plays from the other

The drugging odour kills
With its noisome breath
It robs the mind of will
And make zombies walk
In the midday sun
To await their coffins
Their paths lined with guns
Leaving each state to bite the bullet
Of scarce resources.

The other loads the die
Before the power-play
Saying: Never mind the fine print.
Sovereignty?
An outworn.inanity.
Come on, Buddy, sign
This kind of new-order piracy
Is good for the shores
Of those who ride on ships
Whose backs we'll break.

I hear the echo of Old Drake's laugh!
He understands. He did the same thing for
His sovereign's honour.
"Nary a pirate we be," quote he,
"Just good old seadogs

With a buccaneering crew."
 Yes. He did the same
To legitimatize a national aim.

Caught between two titans
With an old story still unfinished.

73. ASK

Ask any child:
What does Independence mean to you?
The answer is: Lights
Pretty lights! Parades of pretty lights!

Prod a bit
And they may add:
A time to parade and sing
To dance and recite.

No one says, a time to feel
The essence of history
In a way that suggests
That one is stirred to the soul

Imagine! Celebrating Independence
With gloss and glitter
And no felt regard for the price
In brains and brawn.

The day itself for many
Is nothing but a seaside opportunity
As the journalists will report
The following day.

Thousands stream to the Garrison
Or opt for the gallery view on TV
What come they out to see?
A broken reed waving in the wind?

Or perhaps a circus.
For momentary pleasure in
Pomp and circumstance
A visual, visceral delight.

There is colour and ceremony.
Soldiers in lock-step
Whose disciplined cohesion
Tickle the fancy of on-lookers.

The crowd is excited! Happiness bubbles!
Ask! Why are you here?

"I love the parade! See how
Them soldiers march sweet!"

Beautiful music serenades the ear
Courtesy military bands
And vender's food trays
Sweetens the day's appetites.

Outside of the politic speeches
Is there any thought running deeply
From some whiff of the past
That can temper the grins for a minute?

Is there heartful thanks to the heroes
Whose hands slipped not from the plough?
Is there promise to be as resolute
In the day that demands some hardship?

Ask.
The answer you'll get suggests
It was Christmas rehearsal.

Printed in Great Britain
by Amazon

32359632R00062